Jenn Hart is a poet, musician, blogger and activist living in Bristol. She started writing poetry as a way to navigate through turbulent mental health issues. In 2013 she put together a small zine of poems which was apparently so good someone got the cover art tattooed on their leg. In 2014 she and fellow punk poet Henry Raby embarked on the Riot Nrrrds tour which went into both poetry and DIY spaces and was recorded for Apples and Snakes' Home Cooking podcasts. Jenn is most comfortable performing in cramped kitchens and sweaty living rooms, delivering poems to people not likely to turn up to a poetry night. She has performed at various festivals, theatres, pubs, caravans, squats and backrooms across the country. This is her first official collection of poems.

Better Watch Your Mouth

Jenn Hart

Burning Eye

BurningEyeBooks
Never Knowingly
Mainstream

This edition published by Burning Eye Books 2017

www.burningeye.co.uk

@burningeyebooks

Burning Eye Books
15 West Hill, Portishead, BS20 6LG

ISBN 978 1 909136 99 1

Better Watch Your Mouth

For all the self-identifying women in my life

'I'd rather have roses on my table than diamonds on my neck.'

Emma Goldman

CONTENTS

ADELAIDE ADAMS

My name is the same in French – it is not exotic.
Novelty has worn off the lips
like tread on ashen roads
where wives and officers haul collateral
into skips.

I am home wrecked – no vigour for Victory
or to hang these stockings like skinned rabbits.
I make stew from stock and soft leeks
from Norfolk, won in battle
from the other handkerchief hens,
reheat it for each meal
of the miserable week,
slurp alone, the sound –
antagonising.

My sweetheart was buried
under dock gates,
my children are hypothetical,
I have lost my memories
to shrapnel in the roof tiles.

But it is not always doom and gloom.
On Sundays I indulge
in a cough tonic
from the relic pharmacy,
knock back shots to my old bar,
its heavy-handed charm,
jazz tapped on tobacco-brown floors –
the Charleston swept us from white tabletops
glistering with cheap liquor.

I was as bold as Wall Street once,
drinking dawn in on export crates
rusted bronze in Victoria's docklands,
and *roaring* meant whiskey-sick souls, not
the dinnertime war cries
across Balham.
It was always
underground 'til breakfast,

squinting with scratched eyes,
rattlin' cough and sawdust in my hair.

I gave up on it,
stopped sleeping with rats
and now as it thunders down
like a tantrum
I smoke in my mother's chair
            and count the cup rings on her table.

DROPPING THINGS AGAIN

and I think of you
see your face in everyone's
try not to take them home
by 'mistake'

I drop a thought
like a wet cup off the rack
quick and accidentally violent
beyond fixing
what an obvious metaphor

I leave it in shock
sit down where I can
watch it and fill the air
with sobs of your name

CATAWBA

Catawba trees, named after the native Catawba tribe, originated in South Carolina and were introduced to Britain in the eighteenth century.

Summer –

moon paprika-red
used to squat the top
of the Indian bean tree
reefed in green
the colour of ripe grapes
almost lemon

eyelid-shaped
the size of dinner plates
filled the dimples in concrete
with pumpkin-orange castaways.

Winter –

I did not mind the mess it left
without consideration for
our raking backs and cheeks
peach-pinched

frost wrapped the leftovers
for spring to pick like
magnolia popcorn.

Morning –

the perfect wedding cake
cut so clean I could eat
from the stump it left
when the hard-hat said
my bean tree was no native
and sliced through its neck.

FOR UNCLE

Plop,
we drop pebbles in the pond.
His fingers are long,
thin like biscuits dipped in skin
cupped around my stubby infant hand,
his voice is all eastern bells
singing each beat of my name,
Little Jenny.

He is sixty-six and I am three.
This man has been to every wonder of the world
and now we are Womble hunting around Wimbledon
Common,
falling down and grazing my knee.
He laughs in the face of my stroppy tears,
soaks them in breadcrumbs
and we throw my sadness to the ducks.

There are tears on his shirt, both his and mine
as he buckles me into the car
when I am seven and he is seventy.
I cry worse than the time I left my Tiny Tears
at Putney station.

We visit when I am sixteen, my mother is divorced
and he still talks about it like
it's a temporary thing.
I am too busy parading
in my new clothes from Camden
to notice that he has asked
if I have started secondary school yet.

I am twenty-six when he is ninety-two.
This man cannot remember the places he's been,
he repeats himself,
asks if I still like the swings
and I grind heartache between my teeth.
Of course.

I am eager to leave
public transport is useless on Sundays.
I don't even realise until I am past Swindon
that this was the last goodbye.

LYDIA BENNET'S COTTAGE

Bedded on the shore between eroding rock
and the infirmary, husband wakes, rises –
leaves a storm on the pillow.
In weathered boxes she grew tulips;
they bow at the neck as he treads the rocky path.

Later she climbs the cabinet for her case
unused since she unpacked for marriage –
she tips out moth balls, fills the soft leather
with lace and plums from her garden.
Gathering porcelain from the mantel,
all her importance behind a hasty clasp,
she sweeps the garden for bloom, stuffs
the chamber pot with geraniums,
palm against the plum tree –
                              Goodbye, goodbye.

When packed, she leaves the bed soiled,
will not sink her roots into the mattress
like before, on her belly – seedless.
He poured his resentment into her empty vases
and she stowed the bloodied sheets away
with letters from Pemberley.

Now she wipes her bruises with milk,
cradles tulips in her wedding veil,
and leaves her bonnet at the gate
warning a new rose –
grow upward or drown in him.

EXTINCT

We wake to metal twangs,
rise up, find ourselves
swamped by invasion –
reigned on;
an oily monsoon pools
noxious at our doorstep.

I pluck crystals from her tear ducts,
our valuables liquidise,
recoil like singed paper.
Then, silent as tumbling floss,
we sift through sugar cubes,
trudge vaporous forests,
avoiding stillborn buds
like signs of shipwreck.

Hand in sodden hand
we reach a river.
Its nightmares rumble
under crisp sheets.
We sneak across the mouth,
blood thumping –

she
drops,
abducted by
a moment.

One nerve
numbing
moment.

Her parts wash up in exile,
scavengers meet tenderly
and I drag myself on
to extinction.

04/07/2008

I thought you'd be taller.
I thought you'd know that I don't like to be called Jennifer.
But that's how you address me when you pick me up on the side
of the road like a hitchhiker.

You take me to a café on a campsite and order coffee. I haven't
acquired a taste for it yet, I say as I put sugar in my tea. We sit by
the window – one eye on our escape. We talk like acquaintances
unsure of expressions, speaking gingerly about the expectation
of rain and the unsteadiness of this table. If there was an
elephant in the room it would be bloated with nineteen years
of questions, resentment, grudges and broken china pedestals,
the faces I have given you and the lies I told my friends.

But you, the truth, are a sad little sunken man, hairline rubbed
away with every time you've buried your head in the sand, and I
break from this unbearable formality because I am dying for you
to know something real about me.

So I say I like music, that I play drums, and somehow you think
this the best time to start talking about your sons. Those five
strapping boys all swimmers and sport freaks. How Henry is like
me, loves history and drama, and Angus is the only one who
maybe looks like us and not like his mum. How we all have
the same Cornish sea-blue eyes but I apparently am the only
who inherited your sister's appalling eyesight. I am rigid with
agitated interest.

You have warmed up now, brave enough to ask about my life.
I've been waiting for this, rehearsed this, and now that my
mouth is full of spite I can't even bring myself to politely lie.
I elaborate on my pot habits, my fondness for empty garages
and boys who do not wash. That my idea of exercise is running
from the shop with a bottle of White Ace and a twenty-pack of
Royals. I stay out late and curse my mother. I've always been
bullied because of my glasses and I waited like a lost dog for
a scrap of identity but it never came. And I gave up hope that
I would ever be something more than just a mistake. I have
friends, and family who love me, but it somehow never

managed to fill the hole that you walked through when you left us alone in London in 1987 with £50 and without apology. People often ask why I'm so angry all the time.

I relish the fear I see in your face and the way you ask yourself why you even came. You mumble an excuse about the tide and keeping a promise to your youngest sons.

I watch you drain your coffee and then we leave. You drop me back at the side of the road and, like so many hitchhiking encounters, we never see each other again.

LIFE AT THE MANOR

I wouldn't have chosen this house,
this concrete playpen
intimidating the
neighbouring terrace rows
– a proper manor house.
No post or delivery worker
ever knew which street we belonged to.

Your room was cold and lightless
when I moved in and I tried everything
to make it brighter.
But this room was not right,
it had no potential for us,
it made me sick,
unemployment less bearable
and you always slept with your back to me.

We moved
to an upstairs room with a view
so I could write
and you could come home
late from work and dump
your stuff in the doorway.
I fucking hate it when you do that.
I blame the way the bed is facing so
I can sleep away from you now.

Our family is dysfunctional,
anxiety written on the doormat
and the walls are tall,
chipped and aged,
cobwebs hem the ceilings
and a protest of shoes sit dusty
under the stairs
ready for any occasion.

Sometimes we watch *Bake Off*,
pick at the burnt bites of failed showstoppers,
play board games,
hide and seek with the lights off,

20

but more often
we sit behind our doors
like residents in a tower block,
go stiff at sounds on the landing
trying to guess whose feet the thuds belong to.

Now this house is crumbs,
yesterday's dinner for one,
a game of chopsticks in the sink,
a leftover dish of baked beans and spinach shit,
beetroot juice stretching the sides for the drain.
The only thing we do together is create mess
because after the summer
we'll leave this house
become intimate strangers
and you and me
will keep tossing and turning
on this inhabitable mattress.

UGH, MEN

Lonely as a cloud!

Wailing with our eyes pinched shut,
swirling rum and ginger in plastic cups from Glastonbury's floor.
Our clothes pick holes in themselves
as we let the world pick holes in us.
I remember this day because you had your hair cut and styled
unyieldingly straight.
You said you were sick of it long, you felt like a child.

We are women taking up space in the lounge,
stamping dust out of the rug.
We argue about who is Carrie and who is Corin.
It doesn't ever matter
because we are as
interchanging as the guitars
on *Dig Me Out.*

I always think of you as Corin, though,
because of the bug-eyed anxiety,
and me as Carrie,
theatrically stubborn.
Aimee is undoubtably Janet!
We are all too obsessed with
filling other people's shoes,
carving our feet into the right shapes
like Cinderella's sisters
desperate and pressured.
What are we trying to prove?

We play without shoes now
even in the studio
where the floor is musky
and smells like
the hordes of boys
playing the same mediocre riffs
but still making something of themselves
whilst we hover at the bottom of the bill
and tick 'gender boxes'

with our ability to have breasts,
play guitar and sing at the same time

I want to write a song.
'Ugh, Men', I want to call it.
But it's better, we all agree,
to be cool
and write cryptic insults
into the second verse.

Let's write something as classic
as 'Modern Girl'

> We will no longer tolerate the use of bodies
> as props, as triumphs, as things to be lost.
> You have made messes of our faces and names
> and still they are bestsellers.
> We will take up our pens
> break free of our voice boxes
> and rewrite the curriculum
> without pretence
> without control
> without doubt
>
> we will not censor ourselves (x3)

One day they'll write *VICE* pieces
about how feminist we are
and leave out the parts
that make us people,
only briefly mention
that we never wear shoes.

WEDNESDAY

The rubber duck yellow car
is parked lopsidedly across the road again;
the colour is charming only on Beetles, I think.

Around the corner at the end of the avenue
towards the bus stop two roads away
the fog is thin like cobwebs,
stings the angry infection on my cheeks.

Spotify shuffles my mood.
Marina.
Brand New.
Warpaint.

The No. 1 to Cribbs Causeway
comes on time most days.
I keep a quiet joy when it falls
over the railway bridge
on the Bath Road where at it's peak
the city shows it's levels.
I wonder which stop to get off,
whether coffee outweighs breakfast

always.

POACHED

I find you on the wind whilst you ready the drinks,
mine teeming with ketamine.

Your sweat is evident, snapping twigs with tan knees –
you are shy, I am intrigued,

so I dress in jungle carnage,
keep a coy distance.
I want to try the tricks I picked up
in my magazine.

I fall without a struggle, like all your lovers.
You introduce chains,
shave me in public for your friends to watch.

I am the luxury beneath your feet now.

83A GORDON AVENUE, CIRCA 2009

We decide our first weekend will be a quiet one.
We want to stay home and take in adulthood –
to choke the necks of two rusty merlots
(a housewarming present from our mothers).
We sit in our cramped kitchen, Victorian terraced
once-house-now-upstairs-one-bedroom,
high ceilings and dormant mantelpieces.
Our second-hand table becomes an arena
for wild talk, apocalypsed in tobacco dregs
and yet-to-be-paid council tax.
Our drunk mouths run like motorways,
coughing up secrets and throwing gestures of
what we could've, should've, would've said
at those who have wronged us
and through the open sash window
we smoke out our grievances, jilted.

One bottle in
we rip apart the estimated water bill
and sink into the bath.
She paints my face in unwanted papaya cream,
I squeeze toothpaste between the tiles,
we insist our authenticity with a front door key
and our names stuck above the doorbell.
We shove the walls aside,
play hacky sack in our underwear,
turn childhood board games into
lethal methods of intoxication.
But we are too big for bunk beds,
no longer able to fit our legs
through the slats of Nana's stairs,
too old for Mum's lap
or her sliced finger sympathies.
We must medicate ourselves now.

Two bottles down
we make breakfast at midnight,
giddy on the novelty,
use the oven as a radiator
and cook our socks on it,
let our plates pile up.
The boiler's broken
but we're still content boiling the kettle
to wash up once a day
and thrill our skin with pipe-cold water.

MANSFIELD & WOOLF:
A LETTER NEVER SENT

Remember the times
around your dining table
with our hearts as empty
as wine bottles?

Remember the high-backed way
we'd start sentences?
As they unravelled
we'd double over
into miserable bent shapes.

We were bitter then, lemon
sours for teeth.
I gave you
'Lydia Bennet's Cottage'
and you lost it
between Dickens
and some dusty number
I couldn't read.

We said we were friends
like Mansfield and Woolf,
ready to get tattoos
above our knees
to prove it.

We didn't in the end,
sat and watched a film
about Dylan Thomas,
                that wanker.
You loved his words
and yes, he's a great poet, but
I never sat well
around his abuse
                (or any Keira Knightley film).

Did you keep writing?
I want to know
if you're still holding
literature like addiction
because I think I lost it
somewhere in
one of those empty bottles.

You know,
sometimes we have to admit we are those
privileged ones with education and rooms
we didn't have to fight for.

CORAL ROADS

The kerb is a precipice.
I try not to impress my lifeline onto other people's palms
but I cannot help but need a hand to hold to cross the road.
I am searching the roof of my mouth
but the inexplicable phrase is always
an ulcer I have overlooked because of the pain.
This must be the sublime Wordsworth talked about –
the unequal measure of language against feelings
so unreachable...

The sublime:
staring into someone's full beams at 3am
when you are drunk out of your mind
and anything could be your saviour.

The ones I worship most
write their feeling so unabashed and fearless
like the warriors we have put on pedestals
and I have always fancied myself a warrior,
but if to be brave is to step ahead,
claim that light, then I know this –
but failure puffs himself up like a menace,
sits on my page,
takes my pen,
replaces it with a bag of cannabis.

Go back to bed, let TV tell your stories.

Sometimes I can let go of the weight,
forget to tread water
and until I am distracted by something better
I am this wholesome poet
but really I have no discipline, only derelict processes,
and I keep the pretence of control
by being neat
but I am a crumpled junkie with a to-do list.

And love,
it is anger, resentment and jealousy
which feeds this insatiable bitch in my belly.

If only I had baleen plates between my lips
I could take in ninety times more sense
and the damage might be less, I think.

I will refine my wayward mouth,
sift through my pride to accept help,
but I am terrified of being impressed with
someone else's lifeline as they help me
cross the road.

ACKNOWLEDGEMENTS

A big thank you to Clive Birnie, Sally Jenkinson, Megan Beech and Henry Raby for your help and support in bringing this collection together.

To Lisa Harper for your amazing art.

To all of my friends, family and partner in love; there are traces of you all over this collection.

Thanks to my mum always and for everything.

I'd also like to thank myself - well done, you did it!

www.ingramcontent.com/pod-product-compliance
Lightning Source LLC
Chambersburg PA
CBHW021946040426
42448CB00008B/1269